Master The Universe In 20 Days

The Lessons: Building Skills Within

Larry Wooten

Copyright © 2019 Larry Wooten

TABLE OF CONTENTS

INTRODUCTION

"I am the master of my fate and the captain of my ship"

From a young age, we are taught dependence which is okay for us at the time because we have no experience or developed skills needed to survive in the world out there. As time goes on and we become grown up adults, the dependence becomes an addiction difficult to get out of.

This is where most adults make it or break it. You either stagnate at this stage because people we look to, to help us out of this muck we find ourselves in have no idea what to do or how to help us. They often are in the same position we are in but just act cool.

At this stage, they give you their own tried technique which might not work for you but because you have no other option, you take it and move on with your life. But if you are not cut out for that kind of life or

1

your ambitions are more than that, you will begin to look for ways to better yourself.

This process starts by looking inwards, putting the spotlight on yourself which is a very scary thing to do but to be what and who you are meant to be, there is no way out.

This looking inwards requires identifying your strengths and weaknesses. After doing so, you then work on magnifying your strength and working on your weakness to reduce their effects. In order words, you work in what is there, take it from where it currently is and take it where it is meant to be.

This requires an intense realism which many people run away from. Seeing things for what they are and what they ought to be is a strength that if used properly, all your goals can be achieved.

This book attempts to bridge that gap and show you what is missing, peradventure you are in that stage of your life now. It highlights strengths and shows how to weaken your weaknesses by working in them.

Learn how to master the universe in just twenty days and change your life. Remember that ideas are meant to be repeated till they become imbibed and automatic.

Knowing You Are Powerful

You have all the answers to your questions and you have the solutions to your problems. Even the things that are out of your control, you can still choose how to react to them and how to respond to them.

You have the power to walk away from certain people; people who don't see the greatness in you, people who don't believe in you and people who don't see you for who you really are. You are capable of distancing yourself from anything that doesn't motivate you or make you grow. You're allowed to change the terms of your life according to your own conditions. You have the power to move on from heartbreak and find solace in being single or wait for someone who wants to love you the way you deserve to be loved. You have the strength to live without someone you thought you couldn't live without. You have the power to leave even if they got used to you staying. You're allowed to speak up even if they got used to your silence. You're allowed to start using your voice. You have the power to redefine yourself instead of defining yourself by your failures or your mistakes. You have the power to choose the direction you want your life to take without following anyone's map.

Sometimes things take time, sometimes it takes patience, sometimes it takes sacrifice - but it always needs you. It needs your voice, your beliefs, your strength, your faith and your resilience. You're free to see the world with your own eyes and paint your own colors. You don't have to use someone else's glasses. You don't have to buy someone else's painting. You have the power to reinvent yourself and change, as long as this change is coming from within, coming from your own voice, from your own feelings, from your own soul and your own depth.

You are powerful, more powerful than you can think, and by taking responsibility for all that is, and by becoming present in your daily life, you will claim your powers, and you will become one with them. Choose to take responsibility for every thought, every feeling, and everything that happens to you, big or small, knowing that by doing so, you will have control over your life. Once you do this, you will no longer feel the need to blame, to criticize and to complain... you will no longer choose to go down. It is you who is in charge of your life and your happiness, it is you who is in control, and not some outside forces. It is you! It always has and it always will be, you! You have the power to change and to transform your life.

Become A Self-Whisper

In order to address the importance of self-affirmations, one must first know the definition of the word 'self'. The dictionary defines 'self' as the true nature of a person. It is the 'self' which makes one person different from other people. This might be termed 'the individuality of a person'. It may be said that 'self' is the very essence of who we are. 'Self' is the "I", which is the distinguishing facet of our very existence.

Now that we have formulated a definition for 'self', we must also make sure we have a firm understanding of the word 'affirmation', which is the assertion that something is or exists. Therefore, self-affirmation is not concerned with 'I think therefore I am' but rather "I am therefore I think and act and react'.

Probably the most important feature of self-affirmation is to examine how we feel about ourselves. The integrity of 'self' is concerned with the dignity of self-worth. While most people will not be deeply affected by the way someone else perceives us compared to how we think, how we act, or even how we react to a given situation, the minute someone attacks the 'who I am', everything changes. After all, self-esteem determines how we feel about ourselves.

Many people shy away from self-affirmation, preferring to hide or conceal their true selves by being part of the crowd, or by taking comfort in the theory of 'safety in numbers'. To stand on one's own self-identity or to exercise self-affirmation, immediately opens a person up to facing the fact that only they can react to what others think. If you go this far, then you have to develop some guard rail type mechanism to ward off pressure from other people to change the way you think or act or react in any given situation.

One of the interesting hobbies, and for some people, obsessions of the modern world, is genealogy which enables a person to chart their ancestry in an attempt to learn who they are, where they came from, their roots, or their 'I Am'.

When most people hear the term 'peer pressure', they associate it as being a part of growth and development as the human being progresses from infancy to adulthood, especially concerning the passage through the teen years. Few people stop to realize that peer pressure has no age limit and can do more damage to their self-affirmation than anything else in the world. One of the worst facets of peer pressure is that it causes one to compare oneself to others. Once we begin to compare ourselves to others, we immediately lose our individuality, or self-integrity or the very 'I' which identifies each of us and this makes it easy to see the importance of self-affirmations.

Kid Like Believing

I'm sure that you've been told sometime during your life that if you 'have faith', that you 'truly believe' in something, then it really will happen. I know a lot of people don't completely accept this idea, and then there are those who say they've tried practicing it but have never achieved any tangible results. But there are also those who are living examples of this thinking - and they are the people who truly practice the 'power of believing' and have tremendous success too.

Researchers have found that what we think and the state of our mind has a direct effect on our life, our current reality and on how healthy we are. In particular a number of recent scientific studies have examined the 'power of believing' and how beliefs impact on our health. Those who believe they are sick and are going to die will not cope nearly as well as those who 'believe' they can recover and will survive. Many doctors have discovered the power of positive thinking - for example specialists at the Sloan-Kettering Cancer Centre in America are teaching cancer patients how their beliefs can make a difference to their chances of survival.

What you believe is what you get - I think that just about sums it up nicely. Again there will be those of you who may not accept that entirely; but this is what happens when you believe something.

If you believe that relationships are difficult and require a lot of work, then you will only attract people who will make your relationships difficult, or influence you to put a lot of work into them. Or if you worry about something happening to you, you will □uite likely, over time, generate that scenario - a sobering thought isn't it?

Of course that doesn't happen all the time; when you worry, a small part of you is still hopeful of a positive outcome, and this helps avoid a complete disaster. However if you were only to worry about some future event, considering only the worst case scenario, certain of a negative outcome, then you're in line for a pretty miserable time.

However there's more to 'believing' than merely creating beliefs. Possessing a positive belief system is just the first step to creating a more successful life. Let's take an example - you might have a positive attitude about money; you believe there are plenty of ways to make money, yet you only ever seem to have enough to get by on. Money comes in, and money goes out again - there never seems enough to create a more relaxed feeling about having plenty. That's because somewhere deep in your subconscious you may be saying the opposite, that you will never have enough money, who are you to think you deserve so much more.

Many of us have been brought up not to 'believe'; society surrounds us, envelops us in believing life is tough, that we have to fight to get ahead, or even stay afloat. We're taught that if you can't see it, touch it, then it's not real, non-existent, that it's an unacceptable way of going about our lives.

Believing something, is trusting that your deepest desires can and will happen. Believing is leaving no room what-so-ever, not a nanosecond of doubt that what you want will happen. So many of us in the rush and confusion of modern life are missing this element. Each day is taken up entirely at the beck and call of others, leaving little or no time for ourselves - time necessary to create our own future and fulfil our greatest ambitions. If you truly believe that you can be happy, and achieve those dreams you have, then you will transform your life.

Respect Others

Can you imagine a world without respect? For example, walking by someone who has their hands full and not offering to open the door for them, or giving a nice comment to someone who is having a bad day. Doing these things will bring a smile to someone's face and influence them to be respectful to others. I believe that when you respect others you will be respected back and be remembered as a respectful person.

I didn't take respect seriously until the end of high school. It took a lot of bad behavior to finally figure it out. I can't figure out what made me want to change, it could be numerous reasons. Maybe it was all the teasing I did to other people, and later I was teased. It could also be talking behind people back and then finding out it's been done to me. Having all these things happen to me made me realize that being disrespectful wasn't getting me anywhere and that's when I realized I needed to change and start being respectful. I needed to prove to my family and friends that I had changed. Although I am respectful to others I still don't always get respected back, but I can't let that discourage me; it makes me want to give more to influence people to be respectful.

I also think respect and karma go hand and hand. Some people don't believe in karma, but if you really think about the things you've done and the things that have happened after you did it the outcome wasn't good. As an example of this, maybe a single woman sleeps with a married man. Later they get caught and the married man begs for forgiveness, while the single woman feels bad but it's not her, so she doesn't put much thought or consideration into the situation. Later down the road, the single woman gets married and is happy with no worries until the day her husband cheats on her. She will be devastated and heartbroken but then she will think back to when she committed the act and realized it was karma that paid her a visit. I learn from watching other people's mistakes and my own.

I believe respect is another way of being nice and helpful. If someone asked for help, do so with a smile. Because that could be you asking for help and you're going to want respect. I've learned that if you do things for others out of respect they will be there when you need it. I value a lot of things in my life, but the one I value most is respect because respect is the key to a good life.

Meditation

Rather than starting at the beginning, I think it will be beneficial to start at the end. Let me describe what meditation will do for you.

Have you ever noticed the people who go through life as the lucky ones? They get all of the breaks. When you talk to them you realize how different they are compared to people living at ordinary levels of awareness. These people are connected to the genesis, the universal source of energy from which we all came. We all have that connection but some learn to control that connection better than others. Meditation will teach you how to control that connection.

People who have learned to use this universal source of energy have made themselves available for success. It is impossible to get them to be pessimistic about achieving what they desire in their lives. Rather than using language that indicates that their desires may not materialize, they speak from an inner conviction that communicates their profound and simple knowing that the universal source supplies everything.

Genesis people who are totally connected know that they will attract whatever they think about. So, they only think about what they want to happen and not what can go wrong. Genesis people know there is an infinite supply of whatever you think about. The universal source energy cannot relate to scarcity, or things not working out because it makes no judgment about good or bad. If I say to the source, things probably will not work out; I will receive back exactly what I sent to it.

This may sound like a fantasy world but if it is, why has meditation been here for thousands of years? If you choose to listen and learn, meditation can teach you to get connected to the universal source energy from which we all emanated. You can learn the power of attraction, but first and foremost you must discard your ego. You cannot make yourself available for success with an ego.

Meditation will teach you how to keep your thoughts on what you intend to create in your life. Meditation will keep a clean connection to the universal source energy and then watch for the clues that what you have summoned from the source is arriving in your life. We are all connected to the universal source energy; meditation will give you the best possible connection.

One of the best ways to practice mindfulness meditation is by immersing yourself in nature. Take a walk in the woods and hear the birds chirping, the wind whooshing, the trees rustling and the leaves crackling beneath your feet. Fully enjoy the beauty of your environment in the here and now. Let the experience of nature be the object of your mindfulness meditation. You might focus on being aware of sound, or the feel of your feet as you mindfully walk along a path or across a meadow, or your place in the environment among all the other living things. Your thoughts may wander, but that's only natural. Whenever you notice that your mind has veered off, nudge yourself, breathe, and come back to your focal point.

If you can't get into the woods, you can meditate wherever you find yourself with the following steps:

- Find a quiet place to sit or lie down.
- Set your timer (15 minutes if you are starting out. When you see the benefit, you will increase it yourself)
- Close your eyes.
- Focus on your breath.
- When your mind wanders, bring it back.

The thing is as a beginner, you will find that your thoughts are everywhere. You can hardly focus on your breath. You will find your mind wandering and almost impossible to quiet down.

The goal is not to totally silence your mind, the goal is to observe those thoughts and watch them pass.

Releasement

Let me share a secret with you, it is referred to as the Law of Forgiveness. Because we are beings of energy, universal laws and principles govern our energy. These laws may be considered divine laws, imbued with Spirit. These laws dictate the results of our thoughts and actions.

Basically, we cannot purify ourselves as long as we harbor negative feelings of hate, anger, intolerance, criticism and other such feelings towards others. It is in forgiving others that we forgive ourselves. We cannot be forgiven until we first forgive ourselves.

Ideally, when you tell someone "I forgive you", show forgiveness through love and through actions founded in love. If you do this, resentment toward the other person cannot remain alive and you do not cultivate the feelings of hurt and resentment that may be in your heart. This is the law you should obey, for if you do not obey the law spiritually you will forgo the beneficial effects on you health and well being.

Visualize, you wake up one morning and you feel grand. The burdens from your past were removed, the feeling of heaviness has been lifted and you feel light hearted. Your heart is not filled with grief, anger, resentment or pain anymore, and your spirit feels free to live again.

Forgiveness is the most positive and loving thing that you can do to others and for yourself. Forgiveness breaks the chain of negativity between you and another person or persons. If you do not forgive, you build a negative wall of energy and stop the good coming to our life.

You need to forgive because the lack of forgiveness creates despair, grief, anger and resentment in your mind and heart. It prevents us from seeing the truth. It skewed reality because you make presumptions and decisions on wrong perimeters and create sadness and lack of completion in your life. If you don't know how to forgive, it will spread in other situations and relationships and can finally manifest as physical illness and disease within any body of consciousness.

It is believed that bottled-up negative feelings such as anger, anxiety, grief causes illness. Being angry will lead you to become harsh in doing things and making decisions. You might regret what you have done and then you end up feeling guilty. Guilt is one of the most incapacitating feelings to the body. It has been proven that individuals experiencing guilt in fact make a awfully acidic perspiration from their body. And see in your mind's eye, if that is what is on the outside, what's going on inside.

So learn to forgive. Because the act of forgiveness will permeate your mind with healthy and natural ideas, that would affect your body and make it whole and healthy again. This is the particular nature of some progressive natural healing techni ues used today.

A motto you can use to aid yourself in forgiving everyone and most especially yourself is to say to yourself, **"If I knew better, I would have done better"**.

The truth is that if you actually knew better than you knew then, you actually would have done better than you did. If someone wronged you in anyway, knowing that if they knew better they would have done better will quickly let you forgive them before they even apologize.

Become The Visualizer

Visualization is quite simply using your imagination. You create a scenario in your mind, just like a day dream and imagine yourself as part of it. It's important to know that people visualize differently. Some peoples' visual clarity is vibrant, full of color and as real as everyday life. For many others, when they close their eyes, they see darkness. This is completely normal, there isn't anything wrong with these people, and it certainly does not mean that they can't visualize. It's just that they visualize at a deeper part of the mind, a part that they can't mentally 'see' when they are awake. But pretty much everyone has woken up after having a dream and can recall pictures of what they were dreaming about. This proves that everyone certainly has the ability to visualize, just like everyone else. Again, it's just that it happens on a different level of consciousness that isn't normally seen while you are awake. Even though the pictures may not be seen, they are still there, and most people can "feel" that the picture is there and at some level are aware of it. The good news is that the more you practise, the more likely you are to start seeing those pictures with greater clarity and awareness.

The key thing to realize about your mind is that it doesn't think in words. You mind actually uses visual imagery to communicate or think. We can use visualization as method for directly communicating with our mind. By imagining something as vividly as possible it's sends a clear message to your mind, directing its inner resources to make your dreams a reality.

Visualization works because the mind doesn't really know the difference between regular waking reality, dreams or consciously directed visualization. The mind understands all of these experiences as if it were a true waking experience. We use our conscious selves to determine the difference between normal waking reality and the dream world, but to the subconscious mind, they are one and the same.

Think of visualizing as a mental practice that over time will enable you to perform the visualized acts in real everyday life. So if we use this powerful visualizing ability that we all possess, we are utilizing all of our inner resources to help us succeed. At the very least, no one can claim that visualizing hinders a performance, so there certainly isn't any harm in it. Please keep an open mind and give it a try as we go through the exercises.

There are some things to be aware of about visualizing that will improve its overall effectiveness. To make sure that your visualization is as effective as possible, we have to make it as sensory intensive as possible. This means that visualizing should include much more than just visual stimulation. We also want to imagine our other senses; touch, smell, hearing and taste. The more senses included in the experience, the more believable the experience will appear to your mind, improving it's effectiveness. Think of it as if we are trying to recreate reality within our minds, in a way fooling ourselves into thinking that we truly had the experience. The advantage in working with visualization reality over normal reality is that we get to write the script ourselves, allowing us to create a scenario precisely the way we want it to be.

An added advantage to visualization is that it lets you see and live your dreams like it's already happened which actually gives you the drive to achieve them.

Exercise: **Imagine, picking an apple up off of the table. Squeezing the apple, imagine the texture of it on your fingertips. Then, bite the apple, in your mind, of course. Next, imagine the taste in your mouth. I'm sure we all have had this experience many times. So, visualizing the whole process is something you should be able to do with some practice. Take a day or two to practice doing exercises like this. Be sure to use situations that you have experienced many times to make it that much easier to Become The Visualizer.**

Goal Setting Is A Must

There have been many people over the years that swear by setting goals and they do it on a yearly, □uarterly, monthly, weekly, and daily basis. Do they achieve each goal they set just because they set their goal? Are they more successful than someone that does not set goals? Why is goal setting so important and how can it be done effectively? Here are the answers and more.

First, you have to understand that just because someone sets a goal does not mean they will achieve it. However, because they set the goal there is a better chance that they will achieve it and there is a better chance that if they do not achieve it, they will still do better than they would have without the goal. Goals are one of the most important things to have in life, but you have to be reasonable.

If you are in sales or do anything of that nature, then you know all about goals. They can be very demanding on your time, your efforts, and your brain. This is good, though. As human beings we may not like to be challenged, but when we are challenged we thrive and we find out who we really are. If you set a goal for yourself and you have the determination to chase after the goal, then you will probably get that goal sooner or later.

Second, you have to know how to properly set goals so that you can achieve them. When you do not achieve a goal or even get close to it, then you will lose some of your drive and some of your self-confidence. This is not good. It is best to set reasonable goals that are not too low that they do not challenge you, but not so high that they are impossible to reach. Start off small and work your way up.

Third, break your goals down. Set a goal for the year, then break it down into quarterly, monthly, weekly, and daily goals. It can be very helpful when setting goals that you add some smaller goals that are easy to achieve on a daily and weekly basis. That way when you get to cross them off you can see your progress and know that you are getting much closer to your ultimate goals for the week and year.

The final part is to consistently meditate and visualize your goals. Do this once and nothing will happen. Do it for a month and you will find some benefit in it. Do it for a year and your life will be different. Do it for ten years and your life will be greater than you could have imagined. Like going to the gym consistency is the key. Over intense visualization sessions over extreme meditation. Consistency is more important than them all. Without it you will go nowhere with you can go anywhere.

Take this day by day. It's not something that going to change your life overnight. It is a habit to acquire. Stick with it and you will reap the rewards. Remember without goals the powers of your mind will drift aimlessly about. Your mind is a very powerful tool but it needs a direction to go in.

Artillery only works when it has coordinates to zero in on. Artillery going every which way is just as much as a liability as an asset. Not a perfect metaphor but you get the idea.

Go Out & Fail

We're taught at an early age that failure is a bad thing. When we do poorly on tests, we receive a failing grade. When a business goes bankrupt or dies, it is said to fail. We are constantly reminded every day that failure is something negative. But what about the positives of failure? There are so many benefits to failing, I find it difficult to argue that failure is anything close to negative.

Above all else, failure is an opportunity to learn; and there is a lesson to be learned in every loss we encounter.

"I have not failed. I've just found 10,000 ways that won't work." - Thomas A. Edison

This □uote is great at stripping failure off its negative connotation. Failure is simply a way something "won't work". Instead of being a "lack of success", it becomes part of the process of trial and error. Thus, each idea we try that doesn't work brings us that much closer to an idea that does. To that end, experiencing failure is a necessary step in arriving at success.

Keep in mind, it is very important you learn from every failure and that the same failure isn't experienced twice. This could lead to unnecessary wastes of time and money and even possibly fatal mistakes.

Failure, like marketing or accounting is a normal business process. Because of this, failure is something you must get used to in order to survive. Failure is such a common occurrence it should come to be expected. Thus, ensure you develop thicker skin if setbacks seem to bother you.

Get used to the fact that you will experience more failures than successes. This doesn't make you a failure, but an even more savvy business owner. Identifying opportunities and trying to capitalize on them are valuable skills that will inevitably cause failure. You aren't a prophet, so it is impossible for you to know which ideas will be profitable. The only way to know for sure is to try. Probably the most important thing to remember about failure is that it can't be avoided. Trying to avoid failure will only prevent you from acting–and there is more danger in not acting than in failure itself.

Failures must be taken seriously. Because mistakes are expensive, they should be studied to ensure a lesson is identified. Even more important is to make sure you are able to identify a failure when it occurs. If you can't spot a failure when it happens, mistakes will continue until you learn to fix them. This can be extremely costly and potentially fatal for your business. Thus, you must handle failures with care by ensuring you can identify them when they occur. Then, be sure to pinpoint the lesson to be learned.

The culture of not failing was imbibed in us through the academicians with whom if you missed a sum, means you have failed. In real life, there are many ways to skin a cat. The unknown or hidden truth behind failure and success is that both of them are feedbacks. What do i mean?

Let's use an example of two friends with the name Dan and David respectively.

Dan gets a business idea and decides to work on it. He goes out and buys his products, rents a space and gets everything into place. He launches the business and work begins.

Six months into the business, profit seems to be plunging and he is discouraged. Entrepreneurship isn't what its made to sound like. He starts running helter-skelter to find a solution all to no avail. He ends up selling the business and going back to work for a corporate organization.

Daniel on the other hand gets a business idea, gets the product, rents a space and launches. Six months into the business, he notices profits plunging. Instead of running helter-skelter, he decides to find out why. He tells his staffs that he needs time to assess the situation and would call the back when he's back on his feet. Then he closes the business.

He begins to buy books and attend seminars on business. Eventually, he finds a mentor who puts him through and introduces him to more successful people. He begins to absorb more business knowledge and after 4 to 5 months, he opens the business again and calls back his staffs.

Using his new found knowledge, profits begin to soar and on seeing this, his mentor introduces him to a bank manager who can help David secure a loan to expand his business.

What is the difference between the two friends? The difference is that one sees failure as the final destination while the other sees it as an opportunity to learn.

The truth is that in real life, *failure and success are feedbacks*. Failure is telling you that your approach isn't working and needs to be changed. Success is telling you that your approach is good and if improved upon, can be better.

So begin to see failure for what it is. **FAILURE IS A FEEDBACK.**

Racism

I really think that racism is a waste of our time. It's a waste of our energy because it distracts us from all the things we could do as human beings.

Derogatory words but, more importantly, negative thoughts only hurt ourselves. I heard a comedian say a joke talking about a racist and a blood transfusion. It was funny to me, just from the setup. He said, "Things you don't hear from racist, I never heard a racist say, I really really would like to live, unless you have to give me some of that black blood, Yuckkk!" I thought that was funny.

You can't achieve Mastery, thinking these negative thoughts. We're constantly managing perceptions from others, about who we are as a person. I found myself thinking, who cares what my family members believe. I know right from wrong. Or should I say, I know how I wouldn't want to be treated, just as I know the good treatment. Once I began to see this, I cared less about others expectations of me. It became easier to be my full self. I want to do that for other people.

Racism would make you lose sight of the geniuses outside of self. Thinkers know better than to be racist. It's generally understood that racists are, well, not thinkers. It's not that racists are necessarily stupid--it's not that. I can only use my family as an example. They just don't care to learn about their wrong biases. I get it. I think that's racism at its core, choosing to hang on to their bias because they never was taught any better or maybe they feel they needed that privileged head start.

Those of us who are educated or who think we can overcome any bias through information and intention.

Combine freedom of choice with the reality that choices are made based on education, be that good or bad education, or miss-guided judgment or simply the influence of marketing and media, things start to make sense. It is clear that humans have a herd mentality, and think what they are told to think, without using personal experience or common sense. We must allow for people to be as blatantly stupid as they possibly can with following these racist thoughts and prejudiced attitudes. Most are not thinking about Mastery. Humans are like animals, if you beat them enough times with a stick, they can become scared when they see a stick. Furthermore, you can have ANY view. If you tell that view to your offspring enough times, you'll run into many situations to support that view. That's how the universe works. It attracts your perception while stroking your ego at the same time. Convincing the offspring that your view is true but, really you just manifested it into your lives. Likewise, if they hear prejudicial statements often enough, they will believe what they hear, regardless of being totally unfounded. Thus, like any animal, their choices and prejudices, are very often put into their mind rather than being made with objective reason or wisdom. People will believe all sorts of things if the right people tell them. I realized it was trained behavior. I'll be working toward Mastery, not hate.

Quote:

"Racism isn't born, folks. It's taught. I have a 2-year-old son. Know what he hates? Naps. End of list."

— **Denis Leary**

Time Management

Time is precious. The time once lost cannot be regained in your life, no matter what you do or how much you spend. There are only 24 hours in a day, which have to be wisely spent with good time management to ensure you make maximum use of whatever time you have. As you can never store, save or borrow time, use effective time management to manage your time as time once gone, stays gone.

It is easy to define the management of time; it just involves managing your time well. It is with good management that you improve your efficiency and do more of what you have to do. Time management does not imply that you have to cut corners or reduce the □uality of your work; it just means you have to whatever chores you have to do □uicker and sooner. Once you learn to manage your time, you learn how to work smarter and not harder or longer than re□uired.

With effective time management, you reduce the amount of any unhealthy stress you feel. No matter what you do, you always have lots of request, work, demands and distractions to attend to everyday. It is only if you learn how to manage your time well will you be able to complete all these tasks, and may even find time for yourself.

You have to learn to prioritize your choices and decisions based on your values. Once you know what matters, and you do it efficiently, it means you have spent your time well. This gives you a feeling of fulfillment and a clear and more satisfied head to handle more tasks.

Another importance of time management is the fact that it leaves you with more energy. Once you complete tasks on time, you attain a level of satisfaction and energy which makes you feel good. Once you feel good, your body releases endorphins, and leaves you energized to tackle more work and tasks. By learning to manage time, you practice patience, persistence, self-discipline and learn to be more assertive with life. You learn to develop more ☐ualities which help you attain more in and with life. You also learn to finish more whatever you started with sooner and learn to overcome procrastination and thus learn how to not waste time.

Work To Be A Better

Communicator

Learning how to be a better communicator is easier than you might imagine. When you think about it, life is one giant improv show. We don't have our lines fed to us, so we have to make split-second decisions about our life's script. The problem with this immediacy is that sometimes we let our emotions take over, and a conversation becomes more about winning or feeling vindicated than about accomplishing a goal or resolving conflict. While your rage might swoop in, a clear head will remind you, focus on the facts of the situation. Communication at it's the highest level will take focus like this as well as using breathing techniques to keep a cool head.

There are countless benefits when an individual is able to look past emotion and communicate the reality of a situation. Effective communicators enjoy higher self-esteem and less self-doubt. They are able to recognize their own emotions and those of others, as well as how emotional reactivity can influence thinking and decision-making. When you take the time to think before you speak, you might notice that your relationships with others will feel more real, honest, and rewarding. You'll also be able to more genuinely enjoy your work and other roles in life.

If you're not sure where to start when it comes to improving your communication skills, start taking notes after you have a difficult conversation with someone. You might not make significant changes overnight, but you can start observing how you let emotion dictate your words and the times you're tempted to exaggerate or "win" an argument. The more space you carve out to pay attention to your speech, the more wiggle room you have to shape your point of view and a potential solution. You'll earn the respect of others, and you'll reduce your overall level of anxiety. So start paying attention, and see how you can change your script in life.

Apologize To Someone

When you are the one who has made a big mistake or gone back on your word, it can be really challenging to face it and say "Yes, I screwed up, but now I really want to move on. How can I make it up to you?" Because the truth is that we want to go on like nothing happened. We want to be forgiven without having to ask for it. We want the sun to smile down and say "Of course it's okay, you don't need to say anything, we'll all just pretend like it never happened." But it did happen, we did screw up, and the only way we are going to be able to move forward is by owning our mistake. Ouch, I know it hurts, but think of how free you will feel once you fess up and apologize instead of harboring guilt as you walk through your life.

The one that you hurt or offended deserves a sincere apology. I'm not talking about a general "sorry for everything" but rather, a specific sincere apology.

Apologizing can be one of the hardest things we ever have to do. Most of us are overly attached to our ego, and feel that the act of apologizing in some way jeopardizes it. Apologizing can be extremely difficult, but it gets easier with practice. Eventually you can get to the point where you immediately recognize when you've hurt someone, and you can apologize quickly and sincerely.

When we were children and our parents made us apologize, we'd grunt out a forced "sorry." That was good enough so we learned that that's all an apology needs to be. We were taught wrong. As adults, we need to master the art of the sincere apology. It doesn't matter if we are apologizing to a romantic partner, a friend, or family member. Nobody wants to be on the receiving end of either no apology, or an insincere apology meant just to placate and smooth things over. Apologies are the tool to acknowledge your wrong doing, the impact of what you did to the other, and promote healing for the one you hurt and the relationship.

Learning how to properly apologize builds stronger, healthier relationships. It can be difficult to swallow your pride and admit that you were wrong and to ask for forgiveness but that is exactly what you need to do. Especially if you value the relationship with the person you have offended or hurt.

What Is an Apology?

An apology is a statement that has two key elements:

- It shows your remorse over your actions.
- It acknowledges the hurt that your actions have caused to someone else.

We all need to learn how to apologize – after all, no one is perfect. We all make mistakes, and we all have the capability to hurt people through our behaviors and actions, whether these are intentional or not.

It isn't always easy to apologize, but it's the most effective way to restore trust and balance in a relationship, when you've done something wrong.

Why Apologize?

There are many reasons why you should make a sincere apology when you've hurt someone unnecessarily, or have made a mistake.

First, an apology opens a dialogue between yourself and the other person. Your willingness to admit your mistake can give the other person the opportunity he needs to communicate with you, and start dealing with his feelings.

When you apologize, you also acknowledge that you engaged in unacceptable behavior. This helps you rebuild trust and reestablish your relationship with the other person. It also gives you a chance to discuss what is and isn't acceptable.

What's more, when you admit that the situation was your fault, you restore dignity to the person you hurt. This can begin the healing process, and it can ensure that she doesn't unjustly blame herself for what happened.

Last, a sincere apology shows that you're taking responsibility for your actions. This can strengthen your self-confidence, self-respect, and reputation. You're also likely to feel a sense of relief when you come clean about your actions, and it's one of the best ways to restore your integrity   in the eyes of others.

Why Apologies Are Difficult

With all these negative consequences, why do some people still refuse to apologize?

First, apologies take courage. When you admit that you were wrong, it puts you in a vulnerable position, which can open you up to attack or blame. Some people struggle to show this courage.

Alternatively, you may be so full of shame and embarrassment over your actions that you can't bring yourself to face the other person.

Or, you may be following the advice "never apologize, never explain." It's up to you if you want to be this arrogant, but, if you do, don't expect to be seen as a wise or an inspiring leader.

How to Apologize Appropriately

Two psychologists, Steven Scher and John Darley, present a four-step framework that you can use when you make an apology.

Let's look at each step, below.

Step 1: Express Remorse

Every apology needs to start with two magic words: "I'm sorry," or "I apologize." This is essential because these words express remorse over your actions.

For example, you could say: "I'm sorry that I snapped at you yesterday. I feel embarrassed and ashamed by the way I acted."

Your words need to be sincere and authentic . Be honest with yourself, and with the other person, about why you want to apologize. Never make an apology when you have ulterior motives, or if you see it as a means to an end.

Timeliness is also important here. Apologize as soon as you realize that you've wronged someone else.

Step 2: Admit Responsibility

Next, admit responsibility for your actions or behavior, and acknowledge what you did.

Here, you need to empathize with the person you wronged, and demonstrate that you understand how you made her feel.

Don't make assumptions – instead, simply try to put yourself in that person's shoes and imagine how she felt.

For example: "I know that I hurt your feelings yesterday when I snapped at you. I'm sure this embarrassed you, especially since everyone else on the team was there. I was wrong to treat you like that."

Step 3: Make Amends

When you make amends , you take action to make the situation right.

Here are two examples:

"If there's anything that I can do to make this up to you, please just ask."

"I realize that I was wrong to doubt your ability to chair our staff meeting. I'd like you to lead the team through tomorrow's meeting to demonstrate your skills."

Think carefully about this step. Token gestures or empty promises will do more harm than good. Because you feel guilty, you might also be tempted to give more than what's appropriate – so be proportionate in what you offer.

Step 4: Promise That It Won't Happen Again

Your last step is to explain that you won't repeat the action or behavior.

This step is important because you reassure the other person that you're going to change your behavior. This helps you rebuild trust and repair the relationship.

You could say: "From now on, I'm going to manage my stress better, so that I don't snap at you and the rest of the team. And, I want you to call me out if I do this again."

Make sure that you honor this commitment in the days or weeks to come – if you promise to change your behavior, but don't follow through, others will question your reputation and your trustworthiness.

Quote "Never ruin an apology with an excuse."

— **Benjamin Franklin**

Work To Be A Better Listener

People, oftentimes, have things going on in their lives where they ultimately need someone with whom to talk things over. It can be an overwhelming burden to try to carry problems alone. Just the act of "venting" can be very helpful to people. Who they choose to "unload" on can vary, depending on the problem they are facing. If it is just a matter of being over-worked or under-appreciated, a close and trusted friend may be the right ear to seek. If the issue, on the other hand, is more of a moral or intimate problem, they may seek the advice of a doctor or clergy person.

It is very important when listening that you actually listen. Sometimes, people are more interested in their own input and they simply wait for an opening to regain the floor. We have two ears and one mouth - meaning that we should listen twice as much as we speak. If the adviser were a paid counselor, it would be a disservice to the client/patient to not listen intently. Clear understanding on the counselor's part is essential. How else could they respond appropriately? Listen intently, observe the pain or concern of the patient/client and only then, can a diagnosis or proper advice be dispensed.

One effective tool in listening is to repeat or paraphrase back to the person you are listening to, to make sure you heard correctly and understand the issue. If you misunderstood, they may rephrase. With the dialogue out in the open, the intent and perception clear, a potential solution to the problem may be easier to identify.

The hidden truth about being a listener is that you hold the power of the conversation. You can direct the conversation to whatever angle you want however, you have to be cautious of the direction you are taking it.

Don't think because some area of someone's life is interesting/boring to you so you either care or don't respectively. If someone chooses to tell you something, look at their intention, not their words and learn to speak accordingly.

Nobody will tell you their pain if they don't think you can keep it a secret and they are safe, talking to you. Identity if the conversation is something sensitive or carefree and respond back the same way. Match their energy and tone.

Once you begin to do this, you will be amazed to find that people who seem to have no problems on their outside would tell you things that shake you. You will get to know that everyone is going through almost the same things but in different ways.

Everyone just puts up a front to be seen as tough; it's all a lie when you start listening.

Become a master listener and watch your conversations with people go to an entire new level as people begin to tell you things they wouldn't tell just about anybody. You will gain the ability to instantly create a feeling of bonding with anybody, stranger or friends.

Mad Challenge

Anger is not just a "bad" or destructive human emotion. Rather, it is an essential source of power and strength. It can give us the courage to speak out and take a stand, or simply to identify that something is not right.

Anger, when used constructively is an important vehicle for personal and political change. It can encourage us to say, "This is who I am. This is what I believe. This is where I stand. These are things I will no longer do or tolerate." People who avoid and deny their anger can suffer as deeply as people who vent anger ineffectively.

Unfortunately, few of use anger productively. Instead we do two unhealthy things with anger. First we may avoid anger and conflict at all costs. We are the peacemakers, the accommodators, the steadiers of rocked boats. Or, we may do the opposite. We get angry with ease, but getting angry is getting nowhere. We get caught in endless cycles of fighting, complaining and blaming that only make things worse.

While some anger is understandable, the anger should be directed at yourself and your own stupidity and weakness. It's always best to direct anger in a positive direction towards becoming stronger and better as opposed to letting it turn into resentment, bitterness, or self-hate.

The problem with anger is that it inspires us to take action, before we know what the real issue is. Anger is tricky because it's an automatic response to any source of anxiety or stress.

It's important to identify the true sources of our anger and to change our own steps in the patterns from which our anger springs. Challenge yourself by going many days without getting angry or mad at anyone.

It's an act of maturity to let things go, but it may be a mistake to stay silent if the cost is to feel bitter, resentful, or depressed. We de-self ourselves when we can't talk about things that matter.

Be Humble

Many think being humble is humiliating and a weakness. Same goes for being meek. Is this what you believe? Truth is being genuinely humble takes a great deal of strength - both in what we do and don't do. Yet being proud often takes no effort at all. Being prideful is actually the opposite of being humble.

Being rightly humble and meek means doing what's right, even when we don't want to. It means being patient, kind, forgiving and loving - even to those who don't deserve it!

Being prideful is choosing to do things our own way; rather than the right way - it's following our feelings and expecting others to accept them. Whereas, being humble is choosing to do things the right way; rather than our own way - it's controlling our feelings and being considerate of others.

Sound too challenging? It can be. But consider for a moment what's in it for you. By practicing humility and meekness, you become someone of better character. Consider how these traits could help you in your own life. How about with your current significant other or future hopeful? What about in relationship with your sibling, parent, family member or even boss? Could any of them use your patience, kindness, forgiveness and unconditional love?

Be humble but don't be weak. There is a difference between the two. Being humble like we discussed above is to do the right thing even when it is the last thing on our minds meanwhile being weak is to be a coward. To allow people walk all over you, not setting boundaries etc. Being weak is running from responsibilities even when you know that nobody will do it for you.

So the next time someone is challenging you, remember the power of humility but access the situation from a place of strength. Who knows, choosing to practice humility and meekness towards others, might even help others become that way towards you too.

One way to always remain humble is to remember that no matter the height you have attained, you still don't know it all and don't have it all. There will always be someone somewhere better than you. Someone who can run multiple cycles around your so called "expertise", without breaking a sweat.

Someone has been where you are and is beyond that and while you hope to be like him, he is also hoping to be like someone else. Nobody is too great, we are all learners and the more you humble yourself even to those that seem below you, the more you learn and become better. Rubbing your mind with others (both young and old) and allowing them to do the same on you will leave you with a pot of gold (knowledge)

Gratitude

There are very few things more influential in our success than the practice of being grateful - having an attitude of gratitude. I like the way that sounds. It affects our perspective, our energy, our ability to see the good, and our effectiveness at creating the future we want.

Being grateful means enjoying and being appreciative of the things we have in our lives. Don't get me wrong. It's good to strive to be better and to have more success, but it's just as important to be happy for and to appreciate those people, things, and circumstances that exist in our life at this very moment. When we look for ways to be grateful, we find the opportunities that others miss. Often we take for granted much in our life because we're either blind to their existence or don't even realize that we have something that others - sometimes many others

- don't have. Let me share a personal experience with you to illustrate my point.

When a person is grateful for what they have - even though it's often not all they want to have - they gain the ability to see the positive in pretty much every circumstance. And that, in turn, allows them to see the opportunities that exist. When a person doesn't have an attitude of gratitude they tend to see only the obstacles. When a person isn't grateful, they tend to be unhappy much of the time because they only see what they don't have. When a person only focuses on what they don't have or what they haven't yet attained, then they can't help but be frustrated, stressed, regularly dissatisfied and generally unhappy.

Gratitude is one of the motivating forces that drive you to greatness, if you can use it properly. Will power is good among other things however, not strong enough. WHY?

Willpower can often be weakened and broken by things and people around you. It is malleable and can't hold it's ground forever. Sheer willpower born of nothing but the fire in your belly is great, but what keeps that fire burning? It's your gratitude, pride, and vision. Without them, willpower won't do much.

When you want to be a great man for the people you love, you are grateful for their love and do not want to disappoint them. You have gratitude for what they do for you, for their belief in you, and when you focus on that in hard times you will feel the will to do what must be done to earn their love and their faith in you. Gratitude is a great motivator.

Go Time

Quote "The path to success is to take massive, determined actions"-Tony Robbins

Every individual in this world wants comfortable life, they want smooth relationships. They want enough money so that they can live comfortably, can have their own house, car and enough money to enjoy their yearly or monthly vacations. But to have all this just a dream or plan or vision towards your work isn't enough. To have this kind of life the most important thing which is re□uired is Action. Action will give you what you always dreamed about, in order to get your desired outcome you need to take action. Taking action isn't difficult. Only, the first stept towards your success journey can be little difficult because that first step will move you out from your comfort zone.

No matter how small of a baby step you take towards your success journey, the thing which is really important is that one step. Now, you're one step closer to your dream and vision. No matter how knowledgeable or intelligent a person you are if you do not take action towards that knowledge you will never see the success and accomplishments. For example, no matter how intelligent of a student you are, during exams without studying you will never be able to achieve your top score. If you want the desired outcome you need to work hard and you need to take action. Always remember hard work and actions will always pay you back.

As it says, in order to get success you need to take action because of knowledge + Action = Result. If you apply continuous actions to your knowledge, you will get a result more faster and this will make your life beautiful and satisfied. Even the smallest action in your life, it could bring a huge difference. To improve every aspect of your life action is must. To improve your action quality you need to improve your belief system and when belief system changes believe changes and when believe changes you get a positive outcome

The distance between your dreams and its manifestation is called action. The disconnect between 'saying' and 'doing' is action. Steve Maraboli once said, "Take action! An inch of movement will bring you closer to your goals than a mile of intention." I have observed that some people are so much knowledgeable but not successful. Do you really know what the missing link is? The missing link is 'action'. The key to success is massive action. In life that taking action is better than waiting for perfection. Theodore Roosevelt once said, "In any moment of decision, the best thing you can do is the right thing, the next best thing is the wrong thing, and the worst thing you can do is nothing." By acting you will learn three critical things: 'What works', 'what doesn't work', and 'what can be made better'. Wayne Gretzky said, "You miss 100% of the shots you don't take."

One man that exemplified the science of taking massive actions is Thomas Alva Edison, an American inventor and one of the greatest innovators of all time. During his career, Edison patented more than 1000 inventions, including the electric light, the phonograph, and the motion-picture camera. In the period from 1878 to 1880 after Edison had built a small laboratory in New Jersey, he worked on at least three thousand different theories to develop an efficient incandescent lamp. Many inventors had tried ever before him but couldn't produce perfect incandescent lamps. By January 1879, Edison had built first high resistance incandescent electric light just as he desired but still, the lamp only burned for a few hours.

In order to get the perfect 'filament', Edison went from one experiment to another, he tested thousands and thousands of numerous materials to use for the filament, but they did not work with the tools available at that time. He tested carbonized filaments of every plant imaginable; he tested no fewer than 6000 vegetable growths. He was never discouraged or inclined to be hopeless of success, despite his several mistakes. He finally discovered they could use a carbonized bamboo filament that lasts over 1,200 hours. After thousands and thousands of failures, mistakes, and errors, Thomas Edison finally invented the first practical incandescent light.

Though it took Thomas Edison about 10,000 trials to make the light bulb, he gave the world some of the best invention that has heralded the 'modern' world. When a reporter tried to ridicule his various attempts by asking him how he felt to have failed for 10,000 times, he said something that stunned the whole world: "I have not failed 10,000 times. I've just found 10,000 ways that won't work"! He has an unbreakable record; he not only eventually succeeded but established a system of electric power generation and distribution to homes. Edison also develops the first movie camera; he was the first to record sound. Edison gained worldwide acclaim for his inventions, and he continued working even with advancing age and in frail health, amassing a total of 1093 patents, more than any other inventor at that time. His last patent was obtained at age 83. He died at 84 on October 18th, 1931 in New Jersey. Three days later on the night of October 21, as a national tribute proclaimed by President Herbert Hoover, millions of Americans turned out their lights to plunge the country into momentary darkness in order to illustrate how the world was before Edison discovered the light bulb. When someone called him a genius, Edison made the famous reply, "Genius is 1 percent inspiration and 99 percent perspiration." A statement that testifies to his virtues of tenacity and persistence even in the plethora of his errors.

Become A Universal Master

It's one of the most difficult challenges for most of us (myself included): how not to get mad when someone else gets mad at you. How not to feel bad when someone criticizes you. How not to feel unhappy when your lover/partner is unhappy with you.

The emotions of others can vary wildly throughout the day, and if we allow our happiness to be tied to how everyone else is feeling, we'll constantly be on a rollercoaster, happy one moment and then plunging into anger, sadness, disappointment the next.

How do we get off this ride? It's not easy, but there are some things I've found to help. Let's first look at why we get sucked into the emotions of those around us, then what we can do to stop it, and finally how we can learn these skills.

There are lots of possible answers to the question of why our emotions are tied to other people's emotions. But the one I've found most useful is that we see everything through the "me" lens.

What's the "me" lens? It's the way of looking at everything around us … as it relates to us in particular. It's perhaps a natural way for people to see things, as we do it when we are very young. But it's a way of seeing things where we are the center of the story, the main reason for things happening, and of course that's not how the world really works. It just seems that way to us.

Let's take an example: someone storms into the office in a foul mood, and slams something on his desk, maybe knocks over a trash can, responds to us in a very rude way. We tend to think something like, "Geez, he didn't have to be so rude to me! I didn't do anything wrong, and I don't deserve to be treated that way! I also don't like it when someone is being

loud and obnoxious when I'm trying to concentrate."
And then we are offended, angry, or irritated.

And of course, the person's actions have very little
to do with us. He got mad at something outside the
office, brought a foul mood into the office, and is
venting his frustrations. We just happen to be nearby
when it happens, and when we see it from the "me"
lens, we think about how these actions relate to us,
with us being the center of the story. In reality, we're
just one element in the story, and the angry actions
don't directly relate to us.

The same is true when the actions seem to relate to
us - we did something that pisses someone else off,
and then we take it personally, as if the anger is a
direct statement about us. Really, it's a statement
about the other person's reactions, anger issues, and
expectations of the world - not us at all.

When someone else ignores us, doesn't call, doesn't
show she cares ... these have nothing to do with us
than they are to do with the other person's issues.

Because we see everything through the "me" lens - a lens that's not that useful or reflective of the larger reality - then we react to everyone else's actions and words as if they are a personal judgment of us or offense to us. So someone else's anger makes us angry or hurt. Someone else's lack of caring or respect makes us offended or hurt. Someone else's happiness makes us happy.

This "we" lens is a tool you can use any time you're interacting with other people - and is also a mental habit that will help you be on less of an emotional roller coaster. As a tool, you should try to remember to use it whenever you feel yourself getting affected by someone else's actions or emotions. As a habit, it's best to practice it as often as possible - use a slogan such as "we lens" to remind yourself every time you're dealing with someone else.

One motto you can repeat to yourself and begin putting into action whenever 'unpleasant situations' arise is this:

"I am not that important to have made all this things happen"

The truth is you are not that important to have caused all this bitterness. When you begin to tell yourself this from time to time, you would discover a new level of peace you've not experienced before. In situations where you would have gotten angry before, remembering that the person is not that important to get you angry will leave you in a secured place.

Conclusion

The goal of this book is to help men and women who are looking to improve onto self. Everyone is not positioned to receive helpful info. As a parent, a stranger could tell my son the same information that I told him, and it could be received a lot easier from the stranger. Yep, weird. Honestly, the only thing that should matter is that the message is received.

Volume 1 Because I'm Ya Daddy, was focused on getting your kids or people looking for a productive path, some direction. We all want to master anything we do. It's really like putting a puzzle together. Me, I always start with the frame and then fill in the middle. As a parent, you want your off-springs to get it. In Vol 1, I was hard on you. With Master The Universe In 20 Days, I took the approach as if your mom was in the room, and you're starting to get it. Because I hope you are. Don't try to master this all in one day. Take 20 days and work on one topic each day. Then, repeat. Until you Master The Universe. Hopefully, this has helped in some way. Please take action in your life. Be sure to set goals and be willing to do the work. Please, be a positive light in your family and friend's eyes.

I would like to thank you for taking the time to read through this.

I would like to end with a quote.

"Shallow men believe in luck or in circumstance. Strong men believe in cause and effect."

— **Ralph** **Waldo** **Emerson**

Follow these step to create your Wants in your life:

First, Pinpoint Exactly what you Want

Next, Speak out to yourself and ask for it.

Next, Play your part to get to that want.

Next, Believe that Want is coming

Next, Notice the signs of your want coming your way

Next, Keep good vibes on your Want

Finally, Stay calm and trust the process and meditate on it

Ask yourself this. What is the one thing I can laser focus on to make sure I accomplish that one goal?

Made in the USA
Las Vegas, NV
01 April 2025

20377892R00052